7,000 Sparrows

7,000 Sparrows

Duffie Taylor

groundhog
POETRY PRESS

2016

Copyright © Duffie Taylor 2016

All rights reserved

Library of Congress Control Number: 2016944948

ISBN:978-0-9976766-4-8

Printed in the United States

Published by
Groundhog Poetry Press LLC
6915 Ardmore Drive
Roanoke, Virginia 24019-4403
www.groundhogpoetrypress.com

The groundhog logo is the registered trademark ™
of Groundhog Poetry Press LLC

for Richard

7,000 Sparrows

A Poem

Table of Contents:

Prologue (page 1)

7,000 Sparrows (page 7)

Dominion (page 9)

Eloi (page 15)

Jerusalem (page 27)

كتاب ألف ليلة وليلة [1,001 Nights] (page 35)

Corruptus (page 47)

Reductio (page 53)

शून्यता [Sunyata] (page 60)

Out beyond ideas of wrongdoing and rightdoing, there is a field. I'll meet you there.

—*Rumi*

Prologue

Birthdate:

I will start in the middle.
I will start as a story starts
where life starts
or rather, is placed:
like a dot on a map

The beginning is never the beginning
The beginning is the point of verging—
the collision—
where lines cross

Birthdate:

The beginning is the eye catching
hold, the vibration in light,
the coming to

Birthdate:

How is the field reached

How is the path taken
and where is the road
it comes from—

I will start in the middle

Birthdate: June 24, 1900
the village of Bezwodne

I have read, though forgotten,
what crops your family land
produced— was it wheat
was it you threshing wheat
picking up like Ruth
with sweeping hands
behind the plow—
was that the scent rising
from your boyhood kitchen?

The village of Bezwodne
now the Vawkavysk district of Belarus
Poland. A mother—
Bella

Language, for you, for me,
was collision, coming together—

the road that led to the path
that led to the field
we knew not

The truth is—
no one knows
brother, not even you

So it is natural
as you, as I have done,
time over again,

to struggle with its illogic
language, I mean—

to believe our use of it
will somehow make it so

If we, we reason,
hold that fragment
to the light, once
once is enough
it can't be removed—
so the story goes

(After all,
have we not been told, over and over,
the beginning of the world
started with a word

Why then,
I see your reasoning goes,
can't a word end death)

Let us name the field,
you said, brother

Quite beautifully,
you said it

Let us name the field

There
I say back,

A beginning

7,000 SPARROWS

Ελωι ελωι λεμα σαβαχθανι

Dominion

land-swell
water-earth
man-dust

Darwin arrives
on Tierra del Fuego—

the Fuegians,
he observed,
had no notion of authority,
no system of hierarchy

Deep in the Amazon
a people count 1, 2, 3—
then stop

then nothing

no more

Order: the first and last
of civilization

So brother, let me ask you:
What hearkened
the beginnings of the earth

Lo here! Lo there!
Behold
a pocket in the seas

—startled water, startled dust—

Lemkin,
only God knew
what we for so long refused
and still refuse—
even after
a world of definition

And let them have dominion
Into your hands are they delivered

So when the seas settled,
when the hump of dust emerged
collected
peaked

(a the, an a, a one)

and the time had come
and the separation had been made
been seen, been felt

and God called the light Light
and the Dark dark—

at the moment of creation,
did God distinguish
a difference,
even then

The rawest of elements,
divided infinitely

and also
never divided

1,2,3,4 The the
division— infinitely
starts with a word

Rafał Lemkin

Birth: June 24 1900
Death: August 28 1959
a life tended toward word
yet unnamed

Linguist, lawyer, poet, lover of languages
we battle with words,
you and I—
Baals in the dust—

like our ancestors,
toying with something
that should have been
left alone in the first place

but Dominion

dominion

You see I believe
we've been fighting off a truth
you and I,
(and language fighting
that same truth)
a truth as old as Adam and Eve,
Lot and Abram

The truth, Lemkin, that is this:
Circumstance wards off sin
better than any virtue.

that is not a truth, you say,
that is a fear

We really belong to death already

and every day:
a miracle

Wait, brother
Wait
Time speaks:
History speaks:

He that hath ears to hear

let him hear

And Death, the dying,

misery and wrath

sorrow and wickedness

(*every living thing that creepeth*) —

do they not speak also

of

    language

    languages

    The Word/ the word

    of God

    and god

    and gods

The the.

Eloi

Eloi, Eloi
Do not believe

A great mistake is to believe
words are a force in their own right
that a word can turn off a set course
onto a new rotation

that a word stands still
on a single action
that it can't switch roots or roads
that it knows any such thing
as a guise
that a word can, once originated,
remain unaffected
by its originator
by those choosing to affect it

A word
like a machine
is of many uses
bottled in
are a thousand voices
like trapped air they combine
this way, that, form some
solid thing, rearrange
—like algebraic numbers
susceptible to equation—
eager to compose, decompose,
indifferent to quality in life

A word does not stain
upon history
it's a bodiless thing

Do not expect
a word
to fight mercilessly

for goodwill
its originator
its original name

It belongs neither to the dead nor the living
It makes a mockery of both worlds

Do not expect to find
a word's corpse lying
on the sidelines
of some trash heap
or fertilizing itself
on the richest pasture of life

Do not expect it
to play fetch with your desires

It is neither for nor against you

It cannot save your ass
It cannot save its own

A word submits
A word submits

to the infinite and limitless
to row upon row
of hands
tossing this way and that
sometimes with care
or malice

but often, most often,
with neglect

Oh Lemkin, how you believed
Genocide
would part waters like Moses
and somehow avert Esther's fate—
save her own kindred
to smite another

It's impossible to say
whether justice rises quietly
commits a sole kindness
to the dark
lets things be
vanishes

Buckled over in a silent auditorium,
pinned to suffering
you simply couldn't capture

(who was it, how many)
for how many years
wishing to join them

Can a word
give grace

relieve a killer
who prefers work to slaughter

no, no
itsembatsemba

no, no
better yet
intambara

scurry under a tree
the beloved tree
that offers rest to you

cut the tall trees, clear the brush

translate translate this will save us

urwagwa
bury in a pit, strain, bottle
make banana beer and you will be saved
sell it in a *cabaret*, you will be saved

It was so strange the way it was
they were allowed to live, my neighbors
were allowed to live, but I,
the rest of us must die

Or she, older, who says,
when I was young
life was good
we were in our places

When I was a child I spake as a child
I understood as a child, I thought
as a child

Dying is something
that's not said
but understood

Even in the disbelief
you are calm

our fathers were living comfortably
they had cattle and crops
they had salt marshes and
banana trees

but when I became a man, I
put away childish things

translate translate

this will save us

It's not that I didn't care
It's that caring wasn't translated
into any force,
intention really

In Hopi
they distinguish neither
between space nor time

two states exist
a transparent border
divides them:

that which is manifested
that which is manifesting

Don't expect to
put in an abstraction
and pour out an abstraction

The world rejects, spits, turns over
reveals its fleshy, unnatural side

hide under a tree what tree
eucalyptus, by fronds of a *umunyeganyege*

by desert, underfoot, scooping up maize
fetching water with one shoe on or off

the shoe falls loosely
yellow, angled, bloodless
a boy's shoe

my conscience is clear everything I have done

you slice precisely
your cut is smooth

nevertheless
the wound ends up
sideways

It's funny how things happen—
like Levi in Auschwitz
a dot on your card
doesn't mean anything

you're absent
from the dot

it signifies your life
and yet
empty of you

but you're there anyway
glasses, wilting muscle, a face

How old do you think you are
seventy
eighty

the old woman's smile is curious,
expressive, somewhat exasperated —

the truth is
I exist for a long time

nevertheless all pours over

to keep you is no profit to destroy you is no loss

But what are we
if not an asset,
not a deficiency

We hold onto anything
they say three days,
we think three days
they say delouse
we remove our shoes, clothes, teeth, rings into buckets

we, pressed to a cattle car,
defecating amongst one another

*I'm sure every individual somewhere in his plans
wants some peace, progress in some way*

These are not, after all,
unusual devices for protection
To be deprived of numbers—
possession and identity
one's contours, resistance to
angles and relation to another
thing

the opportunity to measure tit-for-tat
somehow makes for an animal form
of existence

they had to lay them out like herrings
head to foot

If my affliction is animal
why can I not submerge myself
as an animal would

Do not say animal as if speaking
of a foreign element
and by that same token
an element one can't
completely embody—
of the fortunes killers possess
even they cannot do so
they are to the last consumed
with self-possession

As Levi says,
the victim's error
is in defining himself
the killer's object

(the sea retracts from stone
shedding bits and pieces
perhaps an arm, leg, perhaps all
but can we ever say
with intention really)

Intention is not communicable
between bodies

Aftermath
is the only communication

whatever spray and gust rupture
unleash, dismember, pummel
unweave—

and can we judge intention
by the residue remained

It was very fine, that powdered bone

If I were to tell you eighty-years-old
would it somewhere in your brain
soothe you, sustain you, remove you

At times people heard explosions
in the minefield, sometimes
they'd find a deer
and sometimes a poor Jew
who tried to escape

Expression is what we mean
when we say landscape—
what lurks beneath
three, four-year-old
pines in winter

Do not sentimentalize the grave
which emits growth from the root
or the root
which evokes the grave

That's the charm of our forests:
silence and beauty

Jerusalem

The ancient capital lay south of a bend
in the Yangtze river
that first coursed northward
then turned to flow east

the bodies, dredged from the ground
incinerated, dumped by the cartload
submerged in water
do not sink
keep bursting up
in a bubbling froth

The Juz-bin Mosque parts two rocky trails
stands upon ruins of an orthodox chapel
the minaret looks over Mount Zvijezda
from there, you call "Allahu ekber!"
and see fields
meadows

even when we weren't allowed to pray
we prayed—
a missing minaret
a hole above our heads
swallowing bits of the Qur'an
looking up to sky

fuck your *alem* fuck your altar

conversos, marranos, Jews regardless

In Malaga, all Christians convert to Islam
were tortured with sharp reeds

all *conversos* burned alive

The Christ you speak of died
the Sun and Moon never die
besides how do you know
your god created the world

In order for the soul to transcend
the body must not be burned

Atahualpa converted to keep from burning
and was garroted

What is denied is the existence
of a human substance truly other

Was a Malaga cathedral once a mosque,
once a Moor's

and Cortes' mosque an Aztec temple

A British correspondent recorded
what was left of Pine river:
there is hardly a building standing
which has not been gutted with fire

My gold stretched far and wide
as high as any European
filling room upon room

How many ingots
packed among your cargo
did my gold fill

They stuffed themselves with it
They starved for it
They lusted for it like pigs

in our noses, up our skirts
our ears, our breasts

everywhere, looking for gold

In Peru, Paraguay, the Andes:
where every grass tendril pulled
leaves gold dust in your hands

In what country of Africa
does Prester John sit at his table
of solid emerald

fancy a church spire

think how a score or two of pretty houses

A change in language can transform our appreciation

Belgians were astonished to see
Africans using ivory for doorposts

Everywhere land upturned, pulled apart

From Vèlez to Fuengirola
I saw nothing but fig trees
pomegranates, oranges

Suchow, a city on the east bank
of the Tai Hu lake, "Venice of China"

I thought that a man might be an enemy of other men,
of the differing moments of other men,
but never an enemy of a country:
not of fireflies, words, gardens, streams

The man ordered to walk forward
fell casually in the grass

Loyalty is heavier than a mountain
our life lighter than a feather

I saw many more men follow —
they did not slink
there was a kind of nobility
in their walking

Guiana is a country that hath her maidenhood
the face of the earth hath not been torn
the graves have not been
opened for gold

The result was a mountain of charred corpses

'Deus vult! 'Deus vult!

O holy land I commend you to God

I remember a pond outside Nanking
it looked like a sea of blood—
what splendid colors

Oh Lemkin, the Israelites went forward
Moses with his staff went forward
yet you could not part
that pathway of bondage
your heart perched and clung
in that windowless vortex of sea
for was there not, after all
another man's fields
another and another's
before the sea caved

Forward or back, beneath or behind you
it was simply too much
to move, stand still
ward your eye carelessly

a wayward glance, a half-hearted motion
someone dies

When life taunts you with a red fistful
of blossoms, sprung up joyfully
laughingly to kiss you
you do not deny it
your eye clutches her slender finger
your shoulder leans as if parting to
the light

You do not abandon them
the blossoms sit gently on your table
for a day or two as you work

though they die of thirst,
you don't care to throw them out
or notice when she leaves you

It is not a very little while
and Lebanon shall be turned into a fruitful field

Heavier than a mountain, lighter than a feather

There shall not be left one stone upon another
that shall not be torn down

Auschwitz
by the summer of 1943

had the capacity to kill 1,400
a day

O Holy Land I commend you to God

save in his own country
save in his own house

Houses and vineyards and fields
shall again be brought to this land

but joy comes with the morning

كتاب ألف ليلة وليلة

The images reflect themselves over and over
The images form a circle, they web themselves,
the holes formed never large enough
to crawl out of

Typhus brings lice carried on the backs of clothing
doctors and patients smoke to alleviate the stench

Armenians, Turks
standing in front of the same market
gathering grass from fields to eat

*All alone with no one around me in the desert I am walking
calling for mother crying and eating grass*

Women along the Euphrates pick barley seeds
from horses' dung

Recalling these stories, do they become real
or remain words

*If we go to Marash again
just give me fried wheat and it will be enough*

We reached a place where water had accumulated
where camels stand
it had frozen
so it was shining
my mother took her headpiece
spread it on this icy water

told us to suck from it
oh, how we drank
we all drank

Impatient for water, there were those
who yanked and pulled water up from the well
so fast nothing remained

Those who dove into the well, then drowned
and those who, after, drank the water with the dead in it

A Jewess begged a Polish man for water
and upon his refusal
threw a pot at him

the Polish man riddled her cattle car with bullets

Was Auschwitz better in the summer or winter—

in the winter naked the summer thirst
unbearable thirst

Wherefore is that thou hast brought us
out of Egypt to kill us and our children
and our cattle with thirst

So with these words and crossing myself
in the name of God the father the Son
and the Holy Spirit I killed the calf

Some of the bodies had been burned
in order to find the gold they swallowed

Armenian clothes were sold
in the Mezrah market
in great heaps

to remove clothes from the dead
is to defile oneself

most likely Armenians unclothed themselves
before dying

if Kurds killed Armenians
they could keep what remained on the bodies

Fortunate Tutsis bribed neighbors to hide them

the neighbors generally did so
until the money ran out

a Tutsi woman might be kept
if prized for her beauty
if tall and slim and delicate
as they were scorned for being so

for a while she might save her life
being raped continuously
until she grew tiresome
was replaced

Women's barracks Dachau:
a brothel intended for prison guards
full of pretty Jewesses

Hotel Vilina Vlas:
a brothel intended for Serb militias
full of young Muslim women

"Regarding the Recruitment of Women
        for Military Brothels"

Comfort houses, established for three reasons:
to reduce random rape of the local women
to contain sexual diseases through use of condoms
to reward soldiers fighting for long periods of time

comfort women, public toilets

What's the difference
the Chetnicks butcher us
the Drina washes us away
it's all the same

Of Armenians:
whole families turned Muslim
mothers married their daughters to Turks
which sometimes worked
sometimes did not

Or the barber who
noticing his cousin among the herd
risked his life—
not to save him from the gas
but to provide him
with a last meal

In camp lines at Treblinka
mothers, realizing it was hopeless,
slit their daughters' wrists
then their own

For your children's sake—
surrender here

Armenians surrender their firearms—
not to have one didn't suffice with Turkish officials
so many men bought guns from Turkish neighbors
and surrendered them

for a man without one
was generally suspected of hiding one
then shot

The only way is on foot
a journey of 60 miles or more

Walk, woman
We must This is our fate

In heat, the young and old
were never expected to survive

a strong man, too, would likely perish

the wealthy might buy a cart for the journey,
an ox maybe

but these were usually confiscated
shortly after
the journey began

the best looking of the girls
were retained as caretakers
for the pleasure of the gang

In Amasia
the women were separated
bound in groups of five
carried away at night
taken out on barges
then sunk

In Srebrenica
cigarettes were scarce
there was no such thing as money
cigarettes were money

a clever boy found half-a-dozen women
to bargain with Canadian soldiers

5 packs of cigarettes a shot:
4 for the women 1 for him

this worked
but soon more women offered themselves
the price fell

then every Muslim woman working for the UN
branded a whore

There were house-to-house searches in Adana
prisons were full

Door-to-door searches
demanding money
hua gu niang

Near the Baghdad railway route
everywhere women men children
partly dressed

The stench from the whole region was so great
Turks complained
their health was endangered
by wind from these encampments

Dogs pounced on Tutsi corpses
with such fervor
the government declared
a serious health risk

Women at the railway
sell their girls to Turks
for as little as half-a-dollar

Malaria and dysentery
can relieve you
from the whip and the club
buy you a moment's reprieve

There is such a thing as a lucky illness
May it not stay too long

From sunrise to sunset
the road
as far as the eye can see
is flooded with exiles

So I kept walking— my eyes and my heart behind me

Moor or Christian
every man is a dead man

I got to Ohrdruf
and I'm walking into a courtyard
and I see piles of shirts and piles of suitcases
and what I thought were baskets of pebbles
but when I looked closer
they weren't pebbles
they were teeth with gold in them

He placed the boat in the Priest's hands
then pointed to the sails and said
'Diese'

Trudging out of Preseka
in the snow and rain
a long column of them
carrying pots and pans
bedding and mattresses
all the cigarettes they owned

water in water fire and fire ether and ether
no one can distinguish them

Up ahead! Come ahead! the voice on the radio said
Come ahead! Now!

We can't we can't get there
I will never get there

He that hath no rule over his own spirit
is like a city that is broken down
and without walls

I watched as two girls a 12 and 14-year-old
were taken out of the factory by soldiers
(They were dressed as UN soldiers
but their language was Serbian
their demeanor was Serbian
their faces, surely Serbian faces)

we were awaiting transport in Potocari
three hours later the girls came back
naked with bruises and scratches all over

they were bleeding heavily
and there was no water
to wash off the blood
people offered clothes to wipe the blood

they were crying of course
one of the girls kept crying and crying
we are not girls anymore
we are not girls anymore

When asked how he responded to her death, he said,
I cried a lot
Wasn't she my mother?

*We should all go home, everyone's living normally up there
they're planting their fields, they're making brandy*

*We can't go home because memories have a long lifetime
and the evil memories the longest lifetime of all*

I saw seven people hang themselves in the zinc
factory—
6 men 1 woman
whom I'm told was raped

They had eyeglasses

thousands of pairs— women's men's children's

the room with the shoes was huge
a warehouse
and in my head and the other guy's head:

my mother's dress
my grandmother's dress
my brother's shoes

Corruptus

The phrase "safe area"
doesn't translate in Serbo-Croatian

it's meaningless

so we apply makeshift phrases
bezbedna zona, zasticena zona

Words are always of great importance
when deception becomes our language

One must kill for a word
when the word alone upholds

Fishing:
at the edge of a frozen pond
strip naked
break the ice
a body hardened
a body that floats
will make the better target

*I wonder whether people aren't wired to resist
assimilating too much horror*

*even as we look at atrocity
we find ways to regard it as unreal*

It didn't bother you —
to work so near those screams

At first it was unbearable
then you get used to it

a man can get used to anything

What's he mean, la-la-la?
What's he trying to imitate?

Their language.

What language?

Jew.

Were you afraid for the Jews?

Well, it's this way:
if I cut my finger,
it doesn't hurt him

By hearing ye shall hear
and not understand:
and seeing ye shall see
and shall not perceive

I only thought
aim carefully so you'll hit
there's the only thing

In a normal time for people in much less bad shape
you would stop and do anything
we didn't stop
we just left them
we just drove
it was too many people
too many people

We remain as we were as if nothing happened
we eat well and afterwards we go out on the balcony
to watch the fires in the ghetto from above

What did you see?

truck beds coated with filth and urine
people stinking of sweat shit woodsmoke
and death
someone said this someone said that

What did you see?

the fat woman one fat woman
When you say Kibeho
she is all I really remember

that will be my one real image of Kibeho forever
that fat woman drowning
in thousands and thousands of people

I remember she wore a yellow chemise

Lord, thou hast told me
my yoke is easy, my burden is light

Like a storm I slammed the shutters
of my windows
and went over to the dead girl
and asked:
how can I dig out my eyes
how can I dig, tell me?

At one time I was laughing and laughing
I couldn't stop laughing
I was with the wounded blood everywhere
and a shoulder
hanging off a grenade a mouth split open
with a machete
and I was just laughing

Is not my sorrow deep, having no bottom

And the Light light and the dark Dark

Talk to people. They're scared. They say,
"What about the Zaire camps,
Burundi, Tanzania?
What about justice?"

for he knoweth our frame
he remembereth we are dust

"They're saying they have something to lose—
some hope"

For there is hope of a tree
if it be cut down that it will sprout again
and that tender branch thereof
will not cease

Lemkin, we who survive
are we not killers as well
do we not carry the dead
by our shoe strings
do they not trickle out behind
like paths of snow in winter
like dust scuffed
from our foot soles

Can we escape the trampling
of a spirit, a thousand or two
I watch an ant's delicate
dance upon leaves of grass
how a ladybug before it leaps
will carefully brush its limbs back
to prepare for flight
I breathe and depart
my eye slips into absence—
I am beginning to feel the Inuit who says
I live on a diet of souls

Reductio

Lemkin,
I am a liar if I say
I inhale death in my core
in my bones
my bones are living bones

You, stranger, soul mate,
who leaves behind the road of joy,
listen to me

Am I allowed to say once
our deaths can't be divided

I realize I have gone years my entire life maybe
without ever experiencing real hunger

to feel hunger is to expect
the absence of food so it is the presence
not the absence that surprises

Oh Lemkin, I am tired
I read of death all day
but it is to my thoughts
my suffering I return

I say my dreams are filled with the dead
of hacked bodies
in a country I can't name
can't recognize

Oh, but this is a lie
it is my mother I dream of
her cheek gaunt
her mouth swollen and gaping
she herself starved saying
"Why can't we do anything fun anymore?"

My eyes focus on the one—

but perhaps this cup will pass
from me, perhaps it will not taste
quite so bitter, perhaps I shall die
first

I plead as you plead
let me sit here alone

Oh Lemkin,
the Israelites went forward
so how did you stay behind

All nations before him are nothing
and they are counted to him less than nothing

15,000 men take to the forest
1 girl hangs from a rafter

40,000 inhabitants drown
choking canals with corpses

exactly 15,000?
this affects your story
were they Muslim

such a number arouses questioning
such a number—

and the girl

yes the girl too she was raped
and returned
blood running down her legs

UN inspectors entered Kosovo and found
4,000 dead bodies
that's 7,000 short of the 11,000 reported
11,000 anticipated

Estimates of women raped in Nanking:
no less than 20,000
no more than 80,000

Three days in December:
350,000 before
500 after

less possibly

(see what you thought to be four
was really ten and a complete triangle
and our password)

And the girl
how old was she
fourteen maybe
and the rumor she was beautiful
and the rumor she was a virgin

will these if proven unfounded
produce disappointment

with the other I measure
to another I compare

*For why is my liberty judged
of another man's conscience*

Numbers without details are dead
being alone

*To the mind that which is absent
to space is present*

If numbers comprise the balance
the balance titillates

*The balance may make the balance true
The balance may make the balance false*

The girl died with no shoes on

Once I saw piles and piles of shoes
I thought I understood the gravity of what happened

and how many shoes do I put in a story
to sustain it

To give one word weight
is to deny the weight of another word

But, you say,
this cannot be helped
for this is humanity

I only have enough to feed seven
so I feed seven

Some 11,334 Albanians are buried
in 529 Kosovo sites

He saith unto them, How many loaves have ye?
Go and see

And when they knew, they say, five and two fishes

7,000 murdered Muslims must be an exaggeration

*It would have been noticed if 7,000 sparrows were killed
let alone people*

12 basketfuls were filled
5,000 fed

Somehow an action seems inhuman
an impossibility of numbers

Let's just look at the facts
The facts necessitate action

*until I can see those graves
until I can see those hills
those mountains
those hills*

(an a, a the—

For have we not been blinded in the past
our vision deceived by distance

Is anyone alive in there? Come out
you're to be loaded onto a truck
and become part of our army

several men rise, believing

शून्यता

History speaks:

Time speaks:

O my brother, the story is like a measure
the spirit in it is like grain
The man of intellect takes the grain, the spirit
he does not pay attention to the measure
though it be taken away

Behold, the nations are as a drop of a bucket
and are counted as the small dust of the balance

If I go into a country and discover, let's say,
2,000 bodies collected together in one place
and I say these are the deaths of this country
and whatever other bodies
whether they lie or don't lie I don't see
because my eyes cannot see an entire country
my eyes only probe within a sphere
for which I have a handful of names
so whatever lies beneath what vegetable garden
what roadside ditch what unearthed well
a country of countries a history of histories
I do not see and cannot name
God does see but does not name

lest he put forth his hand and take also

Oh Lemkin, if we had remained dust in the Lord's hands
if he had failed to give us shape

Noah saw leaning over the hull of the ark
a world the Lord himself regretted

and after days of wandering the sea
did he carry our guilt onto dry land

And
says Bonhoeffer:
being willing to take on guilt
a condition of the action

Two things we carry:
our survival and our destruction
hand in hand we carry them

Feelings of peace and enmity go
by a hidden road bosom to bosom

And on that road God's promise spreads
in his ever-loving absence
in his indifference to either describe or name

hand in hand, alone, we carry them

What's that? you say

la-la-la

What's that? you say

Language is the path that separates us,
for without language
we would never know we were separated

no, no
Itsembatsemba

no, no
better yet,
intambara

Is not language the past we've made
that which has become, is becoming
the ghost, trail and shadow of us
below or above

Do we not reverberate language
like a string pulled taut

Are we not the trail it skips along
like a spew of water-washed pebbles

There is not a past that alleviates a future
not a future that redeems a past

*And Jesus cried with a loud voice
and gave up*

And there is not forgiveness

And there is not forgiveness
that can't be fetched

There is a borderland that extends to both
that reaches out and takes what it wants
from both

language lacks all spatial effectiveness

Do not forgive yourself longer than a minute
Do not revenge yourself longer than a minute

Do you not see
the wind sails over you
the wind sails toward you
the wind has depleted and forgotten you

So why do you continue to speak of wind

Why do you pretend you are full
when you stand empty

You say
I will inflict wound for wound
I will speak measure for measure
nevertheless
the wound ends up sideways
the measure is still in the measure

What are your words
but a coincidental gesture
towards liberty, towards a
world outside of words

Oh Lemkin, think of Lot's wife
she could not help but turn her face
towards destruction

for destruction we think
isn't real without a witness

I could not leave it to thought
I could not bear it to trespass me
and without my consent become
legend fable or myth

Yes, words resign phenomena
reduce a world
turn a woman
into a pillar of salt

True or false
your words are the very corner
and breath of you

True or false
they are our balance

Though they might float along
what Wittgenstein might call
the border of nothingness
they are our wild and ridiculous attempt
to hook the earth

The symbol is not a mere formality

As you measure a heart by its intent
measure a word by its distance
measure its distance like a line that is cast
like a soul that is cast
and you will discover what a word is

Brother, soul mate
I will hold my jar carefully
But tell me
what are ten, twenty years in the history of a nation

I will hold my jar carefully
But tell me
what does one more book or less matter?

Have you not heard
the opposite of every proverb
is also true

every hour, every hour is alive

I can promise you nothing

I will promise you nothing

a word is a word is a word—
that tender branch

This book was designed and set in Palatino Linotype by RHWD Industries

Cover art by Virginia Leigh Werrell

Photograph of the author by Clint Burdette

Printed by Salem Printing

groundhog
POETRY PRESS